creatures of the sea

Coral

Kris Hirschmann

D0125032

KIDHAVEN PRESS

An imprint of Thomson Gale, a part of The Thomson Corporation

THOMSON

GALE

Detroit • New York • San Francisco • San Diego • New Haven, Conn.
Waterville, Maine • London • Munich

LIBRARY OF CONGRESS CATALOGING-IN-PUBLICATION DATA

Hirschmann, Kris, 1967-
    Coral / by Kris Hirschmann.
       p. cm. — (Creatures of the sea)
    Includes bibliographical references and index.
    ISBN 0-7377-3007-2 (hard cover : alk. paper)
    1. Corals—Juvenile literature. I. Title.
    QL377.C5H55 2005
    593.6—dc22
                                        2004017930

Table of Contents

Rain Forests of the Sea

M any people think of coral as a type of rock. But coral is much more than just a rock. This hard substance is actually made from the skeletons of tiny animals called coral polyps. These animals often are called "corals" for short. The word *coral* can also be used to describe the structures built by coral polyps.

The biggest coral structures are called **reefs**. It takes countless millions of polyps thousands of years to build a coral reef. Although the reef-building process is slow, it is important to the health of the oceans. Coral reefs attract many creatures looking for shelter and food. As the reef **ecosystem** becomes established, more and more animals move in. Over time, a coral reef becomes a sort of island of life in an otherwise barren part of the sea. Lobsters, shrimps, snails, worms, crabs, eels, octopuses, fish, and many other creatures live together in and on the reef. They survive by hunting each other or eating plants that live on the reef. They also reproduce on or near the reef, thus keeping the community strong year after year.

Small fish swim around a brightly colored coral reef. Many sea creatures live in and on the world's coral reefs.

Because coral reefs support so many different types of life, they are sometimes called the "rain forests of the sea." This nickname is well deserved. Just as rain forests are an explosion of life on land, coral reefs are bustling underwater communities. In fact, coral reef ecosystems include more plant and animal species than any other ocean habitat. Without reefs, many of these species would die out. So it is fair to say that coral polyps, although tiny, play a huge role in the natural world. Simply by existing, these master builders make the underwater world a much more interesting and diverse place.

Underwater Builders

Coral polyps are part of the **invertebrate** group of animals, which includes all creatures without backbones. The invertebrate group is huge. It includes insects, spiders, shellfish, and many other animals. Corals and their closest relatives—jellyfish, sea anemones, and hydras—make up just one small part of this enormous family.

All corals belong to the scientific class **Anthozoa**. The word *anthozoa* comes from Greek words meaning "flower animal." It refers to these animals' flowerlike shape. This class also includes sea anemones, sea pens, and sea pansies. Altogether the class includes about six thousand species, and of these, twenty-five hundred are corals.

The lettuce coral is named for its green color and leafy shape.

Where Corals Are Found

Most corals need warmth to grow. For this reason, most coral species are found in the tropical waters north and south of the equator. Most corals also need sunlight, so corals tend to be found in waters less than 150 feet (46m) deep. Below this depth, sunlight is dim. A few sun-loving species have adapted to life in low light and are found as deep as 250 feet (76m). But most corals live between the depths of about 10 and 60 feet (3 and 18m). In these warm, shallow areas, colorful coral growths seem to explode from every surface.

Wherever the proper warmth and light conditions occur, corals are widespread. These creatures can be found throughout the western Atlantic and Indo-Pacific oceans. They also spread into warm seas, such as the Red Sea between Africa and the Arabian Peninsula and the Gulf of Mexico between the United States and Central America.

Some coral species need neither warmth nor sunlight to grow. Species that can tolerate cold, dark conditions are found everywhere in the world, including the frigid polar seas. Some types of corals have even been found living as far as 20,000 feet (6,100m) below the ocean's surface.

Many corals, such as those that make up this reef in the South Pacific, grow best in shallow tropical waters.

The Coral Body

There are two main types of corals: **soft** and **hard** (also called **stony**). Both types have the same basic shape. Their bodies look like fleshy tubes. One end of the tube is attached to a solid surface and is called the **base**. The other end of the tube is open and serves as the polyp's mouth. The mouth is fringed with soft **tentacles** that bend and wave in the ocean currents.

Although all coral polyps have similar bodies, there are many differences between soft and hard corals. The biggest difference is in their skeletal structures. Hard corals build solid cups called **corallites** around their bases. The corallites are perfectly molded to the polyps' bodies. They serve as tough **exoskeletons** that support and protect the coral polyps. A polyp builds this exoskeleton by removing a substance called lime from the water and combining it with carbon dioxide gas inside its body. The two substances react to create a rocky material called **calcium carbonate**, which is used to build the corallites.

Many soft corals use this same process to create calcium carbonate. Instead of using this material to build a hard exoskeleton, however, they shape it into tiny needles called **spicules**. The spicules are scattered throughout the polyps' flesh, thereby giving the corals some internal support. In some species, the spicules are made of a material similar to animal horns instead of calcium carbonate.

The soft fan coral has tiny tentacles (inset) that sway back and forth in the ocean's currents.

Another way to tell hard and soft corals apart is by the number and appearance of tentacles. Hard corals have tentacles in multiples of six (six, twelve, eighteen, and so on), while soft corals have tentacles in multiples of eight. Many soft corals also have small branches called **pinnules** that stick off the sides of the main tentacles. Pinnules cause the polyps to look fluffy.

Living Habits

Many coral species are **colonial**, which means they live and grow in groups. All soft corals are colonial. So are many—but not all—hard corals. It is easy to recognize a coral colony simply by looking at its size and structure. Almost any large or interestingly shaped coral object is the work of many polyps.

Hard corals build their homes over hundreds or even thousands of years. Only the outer layer of a coral structure contains living creatures. The inner part is made from the skeletons of countless dead polyps. Polyps build their corallite cups outward throughout their lifetimes, so a single polyp may add quite a bit of stony material to the colony before it dies.

Soft corals have a different way of building colonies. These polyps do not leave hard skeletons behind. Instead they are connected by living tissue called **mesoglea**. Hard spicules throughout the mesoglea help to shape and support the coral colony.

Not all corals are colonial. Some are **solitary**, which means that each polyp lives and grows on its own. Most corals that live in cold or deep waters are solitary. Many warm-water species are solitary, too. Solitary corals often build very small structures, so they are not usually as noticeable as their colonial relatives.

Sizes, Shapes, and Colors

Different species of coral have different features that make them easy to identify. Polyp size is one key feature. Most colonial coral polyps are small, measuring between $\frac{1}{16}$ and $\frac{1}{8}$ of an inch (1.5 to 3mm) from side to side. Solitary corals may be very small, too, but a few species are much larger. The mushroom coral polyp, for example, can measure as much as 10 inches (25cm) across.

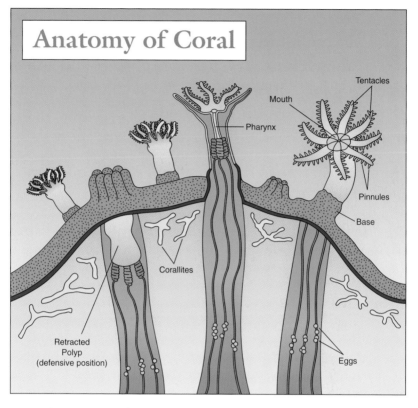

Anatomy of Coral

Tentacles

Mouth

Pharynx

Pinnules

Base

Corallites

Retracted
Polyp
(defensive position)

Eggs

Among colonial corals, the size and shape of the colony can also help in its identification. Soft corals called sea fans, for example, commonly build fan-shaped colonies measuring several feet (a meter or more) from top to bottom. Other common soft corals include sea whips, organ pipe corals, and sea pens. All these names describe the shapes of the coral colonies. Many hard corals also get their nicknames from their colony shape. Staghorn coral, brain coral, boulder coral, and star coral are just a few of the names used to describe hard coral species. Some of these structures are small, while others grow to several times a person's height.

Color is yet another way to identify different corals. **Pigments** in the polyps' bodies can tint coral white, red, yellow, green, blue, purple, and other shades. Some corals also have brown, green, or orange algae living inside their bodies. The algae's colors are clearly visible through the polyps' flesh.

Hard corals come in many different shades and can grow very large.

Colonies of many different coral species often live in the same general area. With their varied sizes, shapes, and colors, these colonies create a rich and beautiful underwater seascape. And because many of these seascapes exist close to land, they can be seen and enjoyed by humans everywhere. It is no wonder that corals and the incredible structures they build have become symbols of the sea to people all over the world.

The Coral Life Cycle

Not much is known about the life spans of individual coral polyps. Scientists know more about coral colonies, which may survive for centuries under good conditions. Many, many generations of polyps come and go during the lifetime of a colony.

The sex of the polyps within a colony varies. Some coral polyps are male, some are female, and some have both male and female reproductive cells. Colonies can be all male, all female, or mixed.

Spawning

One way corals reproduce is by **spawning**, or releasing eggs and sperm into the water. Different species of coral spawn at different times of the year. For most species, spawning season falls sometime between spring and late summer.

Many coral species are **synchronous spawners**, which means all the polyps spawn at the same time. As spawning time approaches, female coral polyps start to grow eggs inside their bodies. Males start to grow sperm. The corals hold the eggs and sperm until they sense the right combination of environmental cues. These cues include time of year, water temperature, tidal cycle, and moon phase. When all these conditions

Synchronous coral spawning is a spectacular sight, as millions of eggs and sperm are released at the same time.

are just right, the polyps release their sperm or eggs into the ocean currents. With a little luck, the males' sperm will meet and fertilize most of the females' eggs.

An Amazing Event

A synchronous coral spawning is an amazing event. Male polyps seem to "smoke" as streams of sperm flow into the water. At the same time, female polyps give off huge numbers of tiny, pearl-like eggs. So much material is released that the water may appear foggy. In the Hawaiian islands, for instance, the annual rose coral spawn reduces underwater visibility from about 100 feet (30m) to almost zero in less than an hour. Other spots known for dramatic coral spawning include Australia's Great Barrier Reef and the Flower Gardens National Marine Sanctuary in the Gulf of Mexico.

Coral spawning can be quite predictable. Some Hawaiian corals are known to spawn two or three days after a full moon in April or May at about 7:30 A.M. Along the Great Barrier Reef, a major spawn happens three to six days after November's full moon. And in the Caribbean, star corals spawn eight days after the August full moon. These regular schedules are helpful to scientists who want to study corals and their life cycles.

A few coral species spawn in a different way. Instead of releasing their eggs, female polyps keep their eggs inside their bodies. Male polyps release sperm, which swim through the females' mouths and into their stomachs to fertilize the eggs. The females then

As young corals attach to surfaces on the ocean floor they grow into colonies (main) of coral polyps (inset).

keep the developing eggs inside their bodies until they hatch.

From Planula to Polyp

It does not take fertilized coral eggs a long time to mature. Within a few days or weeks, the eggs are ready to hatch. They break open and release young corals called **planulae** into the water. A planula looks nothing like an adult polyp. It is tiny—no larger than a pinhead—and is flat and oval. Its edges are fringed with delicate hairs that move in a regular rhythm to push the planula through the water.

The free-swimming phase of a planula's life lasts just a few hours, or days at the most. This short phase, however, is extremely dangerous for the newly hatched animal. Coral spawns attract hordes of hungry fish and other predators, so many planulae are eaten as soon as they hatch. Other planulae are washed out to sea or to other areas where conditions are not good for growth. These planulae soon die.

Some planulae get lucky. They avoid being eaten, and they ride the ocean currents to places that have

This coral colony that looks like an underwater cactus starts new branches by budding.

everything they need to survive. These planulae settle to the sea floor, attach themselves to a hard surface, and begin to change. Before long the planulae have developed into tiny coral polyps. The new polyps will continue to grow until they reach their adult size. When the time is right, they will produce eggs and sperm of their own and go through the spawning process themselves.

Budding

Spawning is not the only way corals reproduce. Polyps can also create new corals by **budding**, or splitting off pieces of themselves. Before budding, a polyp starts to bulge around its base. The bulge eventually changes into tiny polyps that are identical copies of their parent. Still attached to the parent, the new polyps grow larger and larger. They separate from the parent polyp when they are big enough to survive on their own—but they do not go far. The budded polyps are their parent's permanent neighbors in the ever-growing coral colony. They add their corallites or skeletons to the group. After a while the new polyps create their own buds, thus making the colony even larger. This process will continue unless something happens to stop the colony's growth.

Polyps created by budding are able to spawn, just like polyps that hatched from eggs. Spawning is important because it allows corals to spread to distant areas and start new colonies. This would not be possible through budding alone.

Growth Patterns

Different types of corals have different budding styles. These differences may be small, but they are important. The way a coral buds determines its growth pattern, which in turn affects the overall shape of the coral colony. Brain coral polyps, for example, form buds across the tops of their bodies, near their mouths. The new buds eventually form buds of their own, which in turn form new buds, and so on. The result is a long row of connected polyps that looks like a stack of tiny dinner plates. The rows bend and twist around each other into ridges that look like the surface of the human brain.

Staghorn coral and other branched species also have unique growth patterns. In these colonies, polyps at the tips of the branches bud more often than those along the sides. The branches therefore grow faster in length than in width. Occasionally polyps along the sides of the branches start to grow faster than their neighbors, and new branches start to develop. The young branches grow quickly as the end polyps become fast budders. Over time more and more branches form and grow, giving the colony its antlerlike appearance.

A coral's natural budding style is just one factor in colony growth. Environmental conditions also play an important role. And because corals are so sensitive to their environment, no two colonies grow exactly alike. Colonies that receive plenty of clean water

Purple staghorn coral gets its antlerlike shape from the unique way it grows.

and sunlight, for instance, grow faster than those that do not. Colonies that grow in deeper water may form flat plates to catch as much sunlight as possible. Even parts of the same colony may grow differently if they are exposed to slightly different conditions. Each colony is unique, adding its own special touch to the ocean world.

chapter

3

Tiny
Hunters

L ike all creatures, coral polyps must eat to survive. Some types of coral eat drifting bits of plants, dead animals, and anything else that is edible. Most corals, however, are **predators**, which means they hunt and eat living animals. Their diet consists mostly of **zooplankton**, or all the tiny creatures that live within the plankton, which is a floating layer of tiny plants and animals. Zooplankton sink during the day and rise into shallow waters at night. So corals usually feed after dark, when their prey is most plentiful.

Coral polyps are not active hunters. They cannot move from their homes, so they must sit and wait for prey to bump into them. Luckily for corals, there are plenty of tiny animals in the sea. Sooner or later, some of these animals are sure to stray a little too close to the hungry polyps.

Catching Prey

Before a coral polyp can eat its prey, it has to catch it. Corals are very simple animals; they do not have

A coral polyp has many senses, including taste, smell, and touch, to help it hunt for food.

brains to help them hunt. They do, however, have a nerve network that can detect chemicals given off by their prey. This sense is similar to the human senses of taste and smell. Polyps also have a sense of touch and can feel it when something brushes against them. With their senses of taste, smell, and touch, coral polyps have everything they need to find their prey.

Once it detects its prey, a polyp springs into hunting action. In most types of corals, the tentacles are the main hunting tools. They are lined with tiny cells called **nematocysts**. Inside each nematocyst is a hollow, coiled thread that has a sharp barb on the end. A light touch or certain chemicals trigger the nematocysts, which shoot out these threads like thousands of miniature harpoons. The barbs on the threads' ends puncture the prey's flesh. Venom flows through the threads and into the prey's body, quickly paralyzing the prey so it is unable to struggle. The coral then uses its tentacles to pull the meal toward its mouth.

Some types of corals do not have stinging cells, so they cannot paralyze their prey. Instead, these corals send out slimy strands. Tiny floating particles of food bump into and stick to these strands. The polyps then move tiny hairs on their bodies to create currents in the water. These currents carry the particles to the coral's mouth.

Eating and Digestion

Once it reaches the polyp's mouth, food passes through a short tunnel and into the stomach. The

Corals use their tentacles to sting prey and pull it to their mouths. Here, a cup coral devours a small octopus.

inner walls of the stomach have deep wrinkles. These wrinkles increase the surface area of the stomach. This allows the stomach to make more digestive juices than it could if the stomach were smooth, which in turn helps the polyp process food more quickly. Before long, the polyp's meal has been completely broken down. The polyp uses the nutrients from its prey and releases waste, or any parts that cannot be digested. The mouth is the only way into or out of a coral polyp, so waste leaves the body the same way the food came in.

Some hard corals can digest food without bringing it inside their bodies. After capturing their prey, these corals send out delicate strands from their stomachs. The strands make digestive juices that break down the prey's flesh. The polyps then suck in the nutrients that are released into the water. This process is especially useful for digesting creatures that are too big to enter a polyp's mouth. When many polyps use this method at once, a coral colony can slowly digest even large fish.

Even when polyps do not work as a team, they still can help each other to get food. All colonial corals

The prickly crown-of-thorns sea star consumes large numbers of coral polyps as it moves across the ocean floor.

have thin tubes that connect their stomachs to the stomachs of their neighbors. These tubes spread nutrients throughout the colony, ensuring that each polyp gets its fair share of food. In this way an entire colony can stay healthy even if some polyps catch little or no prey.

Coral as Prey

Coral polyps are not just hunters. They are also an important part of the food chain, serving as prey for many other animals. Creatures that eat or tunnel through coral include fish, snails, worms, crabs, sea urchins, sponges, shrimps, and more. Parrotfish in particular are a threat to coral polyps. These fish have sharp, bony beaks that they use to bite off chunks of coral. Inside the fish's stomach, the hard coral is ground into a fine grit. The nutrients are digested, and the waste leaves the body as sand.

Sea stars are another major predator of coral polyps. A hungry sea star crawls onto a coral colony and places its body over the polyps. Then it pokes its stomach out through its mouth and into the polyps' corallite cups. The sea star digests the polyps right in their own homes. When it is finished eating, the sea star pulls its stomach back into its body and moves on in search of other victims.

Of all sea stars, the crown of thorns may be the most dangerous to coral. A crown-of-thorns sea star can measure 2 feet (60cm) from side to side. It crawls slowly over coral reefs, devouring any polyps it comes across. If a crown-of-thorns population explosion occurs, as it sometimes does, whole sections of reef may be eaten bare. In the late 1960s and early 1970s, for example, a crown of thorns explosion around the South Pacific island of Guam killed nearly one-quarter of the island's coral population. Reefs near Australia, Malaysia, Fiji, Tahiti, and many other places were similarly affected around the same time.

In addition to sea stars and other predators, coral polyps are also in danger from other corals. Colonies of different kinds sometimes attack each other if they grow very close together. The polyps on the edges of the colonies send out strands from their stomachs and start to digest each other. The stronger colony soon kills the closest part of the weaker colony. If conditions are right, it can then grow toward the defeated colony and even on top of it.

Staying Safe

Because corals are stuck in place, they cannot swim away when danger approaches. And without brains, they are not aware of danger anyway. Still, coral polyps have ways of keeping themselves safe. Hard corals pull their soft bodies into their skeleton cups during the day and at night if they feel threatened. In this way the polyps protect themselves from many predators. Other predators may be scared off by a polyp's stinging tentacles. A hungry animal that gets stung once is not likely to return for another bite.

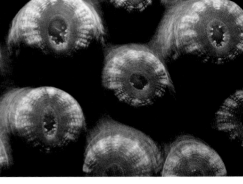

Open coral polyps (main) can pull their bodies into their skeletons (inset) for protection.

A coral's best defense, however, lies in its vast numbers. Polyps that avoid being eaten create enormous amounts of sperm and eggs during their lifetimes. No matter how many polyps die, there are always plenty more to take their place. As long as environmental conditions are right, these animals will continue to hunt—and be hunted—throughout the world's seas.

4

Coral Reefs

In some places, countless thousands of coral colonies grow together to form structures called coral reefs. Hard corals are the primary reef builders. Many soft corals are also found on reefs, but they do not contribute as much to the reef's foundation as hard corals do.

Actually, the term *coral reef* is not accurate. Reefs are not made of just coral colonies and their skeletons. They also include cemented-together sand, hard waste such as the shells of dead animals, and rocky coral-like substances made by some clams, worms, algae, and other creatures. But these animals do not contribute nearly as much material as the corals do. As the living, growing part of the reef, coral polyps play the most important role in reef formation.

Where Reefs Are Found

For reefs to grow, the environment must be just right. Good growing conditions include water temperatures between 68 and 82 degrees Fahrenheit (20 and 28 degrees Celsius), high salt levels, and constant water movement. This combination is found only in the earth's tropical oceans and seas. Above about 30 degrees north or below about 30 degrees south of the equator, coral reefs cannot grow.

Even within this growth zone, corals prefer some areas over others. The eastern edges of continents, for example, tend to be better for coral growth. Warm currents that flow in these areas keep temperatures

Although coral reefs are home to many sea creatures, the coral itself is the most important part of the reef.

within the coral's comfort zone. Along the western edges of many continents, on the other hand, cold currents from the Arctic and Antarctic make conditions too chilly to support reefs. For this reason, reefs are found in the Florida Keys but not along the Southern California coast, and off the coast of eastern Africa but not western Africa.

There are many coral reefs around the world. The largest reef is Australia's Great Barrier Reef. This enormous structure stretches more than 1,240 miles (2,000km) along the continent's upper eastern corner. It is so big that it can be seen from space. Other reefs are found in the Bahamas, the Caribbean, Florida, the Gulf

Stretching more than 1,240 miles, Australia's Great Barrier Reef is the world's largest coral reef.

of Mexico, the Red Sea, and throughout the island nations of the Indian and Pacific oceans.

Mutualism

In addition to good water conditions, sunlight is also needed for reef growth. Reef-building corals host algae called **zooxanthellae** inside their bodies. Like all algae, zooxanthellae need sunlight to live and grow. So the host polyps stick to clear, shallow waters that are easily penetrated by the rays of the sun.

The living situation of coral polyps and zooxanthellae is an example of **mutualism**, a relationship in which two different species help each other. The zooxanthellae benefit because they are protected by their host polyps and get lots of sunlight. They also absorb carbon dioxide gas from their hosts, which they need to survive. In return for hosting the algae, the coral polyps receive plenty of oxygen, which the zooxanthellae continually release from their bodies. The zooxanthellae also take in the polyps' waste products, such as ammonia, and turn them into harmless chemicals. This keeps the polyps' environment clean and healthy.

Zooxanthellae do more than just keep their host polyps healthy. They also play an important role in a reef's growth. When carbon dioxide and water combine, they form a weak acid that dissolves calcium carbonate as fast as coral polyps can build it. By removing carbon dioxide from the water, zooxanthellae stop this from happening. With this help, healthy reefs can grow at an average rate of 0.5 to 4 inches (1 to 10cm) per year.

Main Reef Types

FRINGING REEF

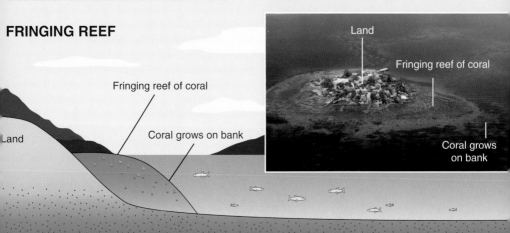

Fringing reef of coral

Coral grows on bank

Land

Land

Fringing reef of coral

Coral grows on bank

BARRIER REEF

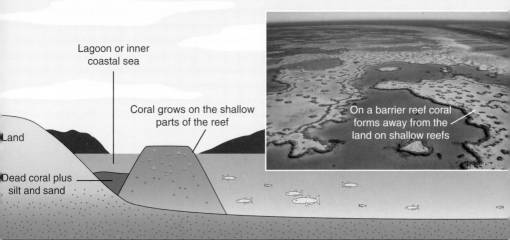

Lagoon or inner coastal sea

Coral grows on the shallow parts of the reef

Land

Dead coral plus silt and sand

On a barrier reef coral forms away from the land on shallow reefs

ATOLL

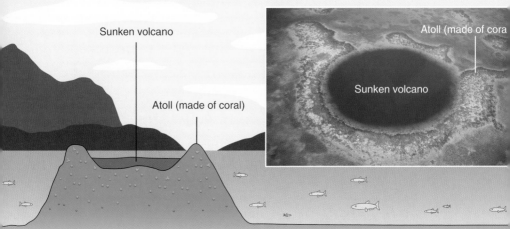

Sunken volcano

Atoll (made of coral)

Atoll (made of cora

Sunken volcano

Types of Reefs

Scientists recognize three main types of coral reefs: **fringing reefs**, **barrier reefs**, and **atolls**.

Fringing reefs occur along the shorelines of continents and islands. They may be separated from the land by a narrow channel. These channels are sometimes so shallow that a person can walk right out to the reef. Fringing reefs are common in the Florida Keys, the West Indies, the Caribbean, the Hawaiian islands, and many parts of the South Pacific.

Barrier reefs also occur along the edges of continents and islands, but they are found farther offshore than fringing reefs. Barrier reefs start out as fringing reefs. Sometimes the shallow land on which the reefs are built starts to sink deeper beneath the ocean's surface. At the same time, the outer edges of the reef continue to grow upward, toward the water's surface. As the seafloor continues to sink, the growing part of the reef is separated from the mainland, sometimes by many miles. Australia's Great Barrier Reef, for example, lies as far as 100 miles (160km) out to sea in some places. Other barrier reefs are found throughout the Caribbean and the Indo-Pacific region.

Atolls are rings of coral islands surrounding a central lagoon. Atolls start out as fringing reefs around the peaks of underwater volcanoes. Over time the volcano peaks sink. Meanwhile, the reefs keep growing upward in search of sunlight. After many thousands of years, the volcanoes disappear, but the reefs remain and even continue to grow. Parts of the reefs break off and build up in piles to form a string of low islands. Atolls are very common throughout the Indo-Pacific region.

There is a fourth type of coral reef, the **patch reef**, which is not as common as the other three types. Patch reefs are small, isolated reefs that grow from the open ocean floor. Found in shallow waters throughout the tropics, these structures do not usually reach the water's surface.

Environmental Threats

In some parts of the world, coral reefs are in trouble. The biggest problem facing coral reefs today is pollution. The oceans have become a dumping ground for all sorts of human waste products, including sewage, pesticides, garbage, fertilizers, chemicals, and more. Some of these pollutants poison coral polyps. Others promote the growth of algae, which can smother coral or make the water too cloudy for proper development. Cloudy conditions can also occur when soil from farms and other industries is washed into the oceans.

Coral reefs around the world also have been damaged by direct contact with people. In some areas, fishermen squirt chemicals such as bleach onto reefs to kill fish. Unfortunately, these poisonous chemicals also kill coral polyps. The nets, fishing lines, and anchors of fishermen make their mark, too, destroying coral wherever they land. And in popular

Environmental pollution can cause corals to bleach like the white sections of this staghorn coral.

recreational areas, such as the Florida Keys, decades of careless divers have caused a great deal of reef damage. It takes just a small kick or bump into a coral outgrowth to kill dozens or even hundreds of polyps.

People are not the only problem for coral reefs. These structures also may be damaged or destroyed by changes in sea level, hurricanes, coral diseases, and many other natural causes. Life in the ocean is full of danger. But despite the many challenges corals face, most will continue to thrive. Many of today's reefs date back to the last ice age, which occurred more than ten thousand years ago. If conditions continue to be good, there is no telling how long they might live or how large they might grow.

Glossary

Anthozoa: The scientific class to which all corals belong.

atolls: Rings of coral islands surrounding a central lagoon.

barrier reefs: Reefs that are separated from the mainland by a deep, wide stretch of ocean.

base: The part of a coral polyp that is attached to a solid surface.

budding: Creating new coral polyps by splitting off pieces of an existing polyp.

calcium carbonate: A hard material that coral polyps use to build their skeletons.

colonial: Living and growing in groups.

corallites: Solid, cup-shaped exoskeletons built by hard corals.

ecosystem: A community of living creatures and their environment.

exoskeletons: Hard outer skeletons that surround and protect coral polyps.

fringing reefs: Reefs along the shorelines of continents or islands.

hard corals: Corals that build hard external skeletons.

invertebrate: Any animal that does not have a backbone.

mesoglea: A living tissue that connects the bodies of soft coral polyps.

mutualism: A relationship in which two different species help each other.

nematocysts: Stinging cells that line a coral polyp's tentacles.

patch reef: A small, isolated reef that grows from the open ocean floor.

pigments: Materials that color the tissues of plants or animals.

pinnules: Side branches that stick off a coral polyp's tentacles.

planulae: The free-swimming larval stage of a coral polyps.

predators: Animals that hunt other animals for food.

reefs: Collections of coral colonies at or near the water's surface.

soft corals: Corals that create hard needles within their flesh instead of hard external skeletons.

solitary: Living and growing alone.

spawning: Releasing eggs and sperm into the water.

spicules: Hard needles scattered throughout the flesh of soft corals.

stony corals: Another name for hard corals.

synchronous spawners: Creatures that release eggs and sperm at the same time.

tentacles: Fleshy growths around a coral polyp's mouth.

zooplankton: Tiny creatures that live within the plankton.

zooxanthellae: Algae that live within the flesh of reef-building corals.

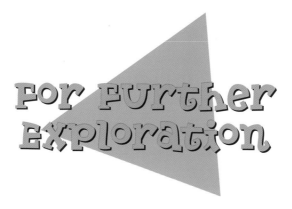

Books

Bobbie Kalman, *Life in the Coral Reef.* New York: Crabtree, 1996. Examines the plants and animals that live in a coral reef ecosystem.

William Sargent, *Night Reef: Dusk to Dawn on a Coral Reef.* New York: Franklin Watts, 1991. A beautifully photographed book about the creatures that inhabit the coral reef at night.

Sharon Sharth, *Sea Jellies: From Corals to Jellyfish.* New York: Franklin Watts, 2002. Looks at corals and their relatives, including jellyfish, sea anemones, and more.

Charles Sheppard, *Coral Reefs: Ecology, Threats, and Conservation.* Stillwater, MN: Voyageur, 2002. Takes a closer look at some of the things putting today's coral reefs in danger.

Julian Sprung, *Corals: A Quick Reference Guide.* Coconut Grove, FL: Ricordea, 1999. This identification guide is packed with gorgeous photographs of corals from around the world.

Periodicals

James A. Sugar, "Starfish Threaten Pacific Reefs." *National Geographic,* March 1970. Read about the crown-of-thorns population explosion that ravaged Guam's reefs in the late 1960s and early 1970s.

Web Sites

Coral (www.enchantedlearning.com/subjects/invertebrates/coral/Coralprintout.shtml). This page has a coral anatomy diagram to print out and color.

The Coral Reef Alliance (www.coralreefalliance.org). This organization is devoted to protecting coral reefs around the world. Its Web site includes an overview of coral reefs, a literature reference guide, and a fabulous photo bank with coral pictures that may be downloaded at no charge.

Corals and Coral Reefs (www.seaworld.org/info books/Coral). A fabulous resource with information about all types of corals and reefs.

Index

picture credits

about the author

Kris Hirschmann has written more than one hundred books for children. She is the president of The Wordshop, a business that provides a variety of writing and editorial services. She holds a bachelor's degree in psychology from Dartmouth College in Hanover, New Hampshire. Hirschmann lives just outside Orlando, Florida, with her husband Michael and her daughters, Nikki and Erika.